CANTER

SCENES FROM

The Railway

ABOVE: *A view of the Canterbury and Whitstable Railway from the Tyler Hill tunnel entrance taken on the opening day, 3 May 1830. The North Lane Station can be seen in the distance.*

The railways brought to Victorian Canterbury a new era of prosperity with their fast and cheap links with neighbouring towns and London. The first route was between the coastal fishing town of Whitstable and a station in North Lane. Opened to popular acclaim in 1830 the 'Crab and Winkle Line' was the first passenger railway in Southern England and only the third in England. The steam engine Invicta – built by Stephenson – pulled the carriages into Whitstable. The engine is preserved in the city's Heritage Museum in Stour Street. By 1846 Canterbury had a new line to Ashford with its station just outside the Westgate.

As the railways boomed another company – the East Kent Railway – opened its line in 1860 to a new station at Wincheap. Finally, the short-lived Elham Valley Line opened in 1889 with its station in South Canterbury where the Kent and Canterbury Hospital stands today.

TOP: *The new level crossing in St. Dunstan's St in 1846. On the left is the 'House of Agnes' made famous by Charles Dickens in David Copperfield.*

CENTRE: *This illustration by Louis Raze shows the Canterbury West Station shortly after its opening in 1846. It linked the city with Ashford and Ramsgate.*

BOTTOM: *A 1906 South Eastern and Chatham Railway tank engine.*

TOP LEFT: *Robert Brett in 1910 steering a 'Burrell' steam traction engine. The gabled building behind him is now Lloyds Bank.*

TOP RIGHT: *Wootton's Stores in St. Dunstan's St. The shop was formerly part of an old inn known as The Star.*

BOTTOM RIGHT: *The Star Inn can be seen in the background. On the left is Walter Cozen's 'Old Canterbury Baths'.*

BOTTOM LEFT: *In 1897 Barnum and Bailey's Circus came to the city; elephants here are near the Westgate.*

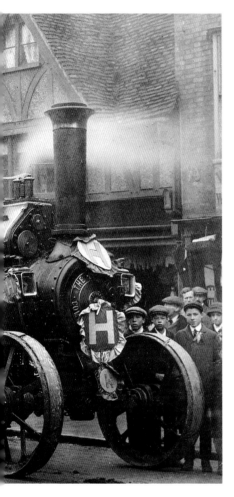

For centuries pilgrims have travelled down St. Dunstan's Street towards the Westgate. Originally large inns lined both sides of the street and pilgrims would rest as the curfew bell sounded and the great gates closed. The Falstaff Inn is one of the few inns to remain. The gate of the Roper family's mansion also survives, opposite St. Dunstan's Church. Sir Thomas More's daughter married John Roper and it was to the church that she brought the statesman's head after his execution in 1535. Later, in 1785, Flints set up a brewery on the site. In 1908 a local builder opened a museum and swimming baths in a timber-framed building which he had dismantled and moved from Upper Bridge Street and rebuilt on the corner of St. Dunstan's and Station Road West.

OPPOSITE: *This lively view of St. Dunstan's St was drawn by William Bartlett in 1828. The gabled building on the right is now Lloyds Bank and the building opposite is on the corner of North Lane.*

TOP: *Captain Pidduck and his Canterbury Volunteer Fire Brigade are shown rounding the Westgate on their way to a huge fire at the Cathedral on the 3 September 1872.*

BOTTOM: *This view shows St. Dunstan's looking down towards the ancient Westgate. On the left is the famous Falstaff Tavern, originally called The White Hart. It was here pilgrims would stay if they arrived after the city gates had closed.*

The picturesque view of shops and inns leading to the gateway has always been popular with artists and photographers. Westgate is the last survivor of a number of gates in the city wall. Most gateways were demolished in the zeal of the Georgian era when an Act was introduced to repave the city and widen its roads. Right up until 1825 the fate of the Westgate was in balance. The nearby Holy Cross Church, now used as the Guildhall, originally formed part of an earlier gate. This was replaced in 1380 by the new Westgate which when built also boasted a drawbridge and portcullis.

TOP: *This photograph taken in April 1906 shows a Clarkson 'Chelmsford' bus in the High St at the start of a service which ran from the Fleur de Lys Inn to the new Dolphin Hotel in Herne Bay. The Herne Bay and East Kent Omnibus Company, run by the Wacher family, was eventually taken over by the East Kent Bus Company.*

BOTTOM: *East Kent bus station is shown here in 1932. With the expansion of services it was later re-sited in 1957 on the other side of the city in St. George's Lane.*

With the amalgamation of the small private bus operators into the East Kent Bus Company, a new bus station was opened in St. Peter's Place, near the Westgate, in 1916. One of its buses can be seen (above left) on its way to the station. Flooding was a constant problem in the St. Peter's area – in 1776 many people were drowned when the river burst its banks by the Westgate Mill. St. Peter's Street had its fair share of pilgrim inns. There were also two large flint gateways, leading to the monasteries of the Blackfriars (founded in 1220) and the Greyfriars (founded 1224). This was a popular area with the people escaping from religious persecution on the Continent. They brought with them many skills, the most important of which was weaving.

TOP: *On Boxing Day night in 1927 Canterbury suffered one of its worst floods; an East Kent bus ploughs its way down St. Peter's Place.*
BOTTOM: *St. Peter's St in 1905 with Saunders Bakery on the left and Heaths the tobacconist on the right.*

St. Peter's Street

The famous Canterbury Weavers House, which stands by the East-bridge at the top of St. Peter's Street, is a fine example of one of the many buildings where the Huguenot families lived and worked. Until the beginning of this century many of their descendants – with names like Lepine, Goulden, Lefevre and Welby – still lived and worked in the area.

Opposite the Weavers is the Eastbridge Hospital, which was founded for the use of pilgrims shortly after the murder of Archbishop Becket in 1170. Later the hospital became a school and part of it today is an almshouse. Across the road and on the other side of the river from the Weavers stood the King's Mill. For centuries it provided an important source of income to the City Fathers. It was pulled down in 1800 and replaced by a house – now a doctor's surgery.

At the other end of the street, opposite the Westgate, George Barrett opened the doors of one of the country's first garages in 1903. He soon extended his business into adjoining properties in the street. Canterbury's first cinema – The Electric Theatre – opened in part of the old King's Arms tavern in 1911.

TOP LEFT: *George Saunders proudly stands in the doorway of his new shop in 1899. He lived and worked here until 1937.*

BOTTOM LEFT: *Canterbury's first cinema opened its doors in 1911. Its ornate canopy was built into the centre of the ancient Kings Arms.*

TOP RIGHT: *The Weavers in 1906 at its most picturesque. Upstairs visitors could see ladies weaving their cloths.*

BOTTOM RIGHT: *A branch of the River Stour passes through the centre of the city and goes under the East Bridge. This view is higher up, by the Grey Friars, with the Poor Priests' Hospital in the background.*

TOP: *The great Canterbury artist Thomas Sidney Cooper drew this view of the High St in 1827. To the right is the George and Dragon – a famous coaching inn.*

BOTTOM RIGHT: *The old George and Dragon shortly before its demolition in 1897.*

BOTTOM LEFT: *The amazing ornate front of the Beaney Institute here seen in 1906. The building to the left was an outfitters run by Hart and Co. On the right is the Medical Hall occupied by Lander and Smith, Chemists and Opticians.*

A number of large coaching inns once dominated the High Street. The most important was the George and Dragon, which at the peak of the coaching era was the arrival and departure point for nineteen different carriers. As the coaching trade declined in the face of competition from the railways, the inns fell into neglect. The George and Dragon was demolished in 1897 to make

LEFT: *The High St as it appeared in the summer of 1905. To the right is the neo-classical fronted Guildhall. This was the centre of local government since the middle ages. To the left, at 39–40 High St, Henry Goulden sold sheet music, pianos, stationery and fancy goods.*

High Street, Canterbury.

way for the Beaney Institute, the city's museum and library. For centuries the City Council had met in the medieval Guildhall at the corner of the High Street and Guildhall Street. It was demolished – despite a public outcry – in 1952. Shortly after, the ancient Fleur de Lys Inn, on the opposite side, met the same fate.

More than a century before, the old Red Lion Inn had been demolished to create Guildhall Street, linking the High Street with Palace Street. Further along the High Street was the Bread Market, held next to St. Mary Bredman Church which itself was demolished at the turn of the century. The finest building still standing in the High Street is the Elizabethan Guest House, named after a tradition that Queen Elizabeth I met her suitor, the *duc d*'Alençon, here in 1573.

ABOVE: *Edwardian Canterbury. The large hanging sign depicting a 'Pilgrim's Bottel' projects from the famous Elizabethan Guest House built by Prior Chillenden in the 15th century.*

OPPOSITE: *This picturesque view of one of the most historic sites in England was painted by E. Smith in 1846. On the left is the famous hostelry the Chequer of Hope.*

LEFT: *The famous Rose Hotel and opposite Taylor Brothers, the corn and seed merchants, in the 1920s. Both buildings were lost in the war.*

BELOW: *Butchery Lane in 1910 showing the cathedral's Bell Harry Tower covered with scaffolding. The buildings to the right were all lost in 1942.*

Mercery Lane is one of the most picturesque in England, with its mixture of old buildings leading the eye to the magnificent Christ Church Gateway and the Cathedral beyond. Its name dates back to the 12th century and under its arcades mercers would sell their wares to the pilgrims.

The west side of the lane originally formed part of a huge inn which fronted the High Street. The inn was made famous as the Chequer of Hope in Chaucer's *Canterbury Tales*. Only parts of the inn now remain – most of it was destroyed in a fire in 1865. Butchery Lane had, in earlier centuries, been the centre for the meat trade and still had four butcher's shops at the turn of this century.

All the buildings along one side of the lane were lost during the extensive bombing in 1942.

Linking the two lanes is The Parade, which formerly had a narrow island of buildings in its middle containing St. Andrew's Church, a medieval water conduit and the Corn Shambles. These were all re-sited in the 18th century when the streets were tidied up to relieve traffic congestion.

Shopping

Many family businesses prospered during the last century, making Canterbury a premier shopping centre long before the arrival of the chain stores. The largest Canterbury store was Finns, in St. Margaret's Street. This Harrods of Kent offered a range of goods in several different departments and adjoining buildings.

Largest Variety.

Tea, Coffee, Cocoa, Grocery, Fruits, Provisions, Italian Goods, Confectionery, Aerated Waters, Drugs, Homoeopathic and Patent Medicines.

Lowest Prices.

Highest Quality.

Ironmongery, Bedding, Turnery, Hats and Matting, Brooms and Brushes, Travelling Requisites, Toilet &c. Fancy Articles, Ladies' Waiting Room.

Open to all.

FREDERICK FINN & SONS, LTD., 22, 23 and 24, St Margaret's Street, CANTERBURY.

TOP: *In 1898 Finns produced this advertisement which shows the huge range of goods and services they offered.*
CENTRE: *A glimpse of one of the store's counters in 1910.*
BOTTOM: *All these buildings apart from the church tower were lost during the 1942 bombing raid.*

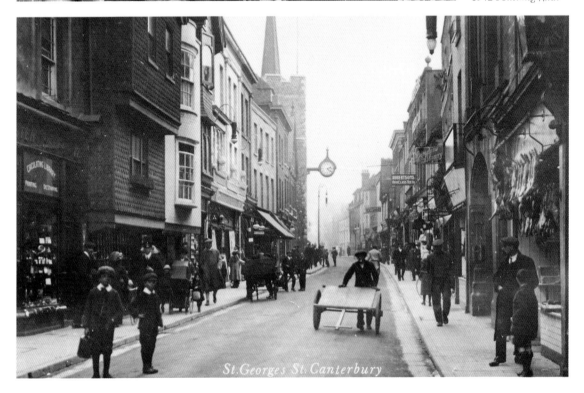

St. Georges St. Canterbury

Before the age of steam, coaches used Canterbury as a stopover to London or the coast and many large hotels served their needs. They included the George and Dragon in the High Street, the Fountain Inn in St. Margaret's Street and the Queen's Head (Three Tuns) in Watling Street. Queen Victoria's stay at the Fountain led to the addition of Royal to its name not very long after.

Other inns included The Fleece, Bakers' Temperance Hotel – which bore a shield on its front with the date 1632 – and The Rose Inn, which was at the corner of Rose Lane and The Parade. In 1832 The Rose was the scene of a speech by the self-styled workers' leader 'Sir' William Courtney, who roused the masses and eventually met his death at the infamous Battle of Bossenden Wood – the last battle fought on English soil.

TOP LEFT: The scene in 1832 when Courtney delivered his speech at the Rose Inn.
TOP RIGHT: A poster detailing coaches leaving the Rose Inn.
BOTTOM: An early photo of a coach that ran from the Rose Inn to the Cliftonville Hotel in Margate.

The High Street, 18-19 Canterbury

The Edwardian splendour of Canterbury's St. George's Street was to be almost wiped from the face of the city during the 1942 Baedecker raid. One of the major losses was the Corn Exchange, which formed a large covered market stretching through to Burgate. Built in 1824 it was to become a general market selling all types of meat and produce. St. George's Street gets its name from the St. George's Gate, or Newingate, at the top of the street. Built in 1380 the gateway was a smaller version of the surviving Westgate. Because of its narrowness it restricted access and was eventually demolished in 1801.

TOP: *Two of Canterbury's largest hotels – Bakers' Temperance and The Rose are on the left. Opposite is the Corn Exchange under which was a long covered market. All these buildings were lost during the last war.*

BOTTOM: *The scene of destruction after the bombing raid of 1 June 1942 when most of St. George's St was destroyed. One of the few survivors was Marks & Spencer whose classical front can be seen in the centre.*

TOP: *This dramatic view of the junction of St. George's St with Bridge St was drawn in 1857 by G. A. Burn. Ginders, on the corner of St. George's St, proposed building an iron theatre at the entrance to the market, but sadly it was never built.*

BOTTOM: *The cattle market was the centre for farmers from all over East Kent. Beyond the iron railings shown in this photograph was St. George's Terrace, now the site of the bus station. In the distance is Fisk-Moores who produced many of the finest postcards.*

TOP: *A horse-drawn omnibus takes its passengers along Upper Bridge St at the turn of the century.*

BOTTOM: *A long lost era; now part of the city's busy ring road.*

For a thousand years a market had been held on this site, just outside the city walls by St. George's Gate. It must have been a colourful and exciting part of Canterbury life. In *David Copperfield* Dickens describes Betsy Trotwood 'insinuating her grey pony among the carts, baskets, vegetables and hickster's goods'. Every year, in October, the market site was the scene of the three-day Jack and Joan's Fair, mainly for the hiring of servants. The market moved from St. George's to St. Stephen's in the early 1960s to make way for the ring road.

The prehistoric mound of Dane John was reshaped and the grounds landscaped in 1790. From that time on it became one of the city's most popular attractions with its fine views over Canterbury and the Cathedral. In 1905 the gardens were extended by turning the former city ditch, just outside the wall, into a pleasure ground. Features included a capstan from Nelson's flag ship HMS *Foudroyant*, old millstones, a First World War tank, peacocks and the Invicta steam engine, which had pulled traffic on the Canterbury to Whitstable railway. The gardens have now been replaced with the ring road.

TOP: *An 1856 view of the Dane John Gardens by Louis Raze.*

BOTTOM: *In 1906 the famous Invicta steam engine was returned to the city. It stood on a site by the Riding Gate.*

LEFT: *This early view of the Longport shows St. Augustine's cemetery gate in the distance. In the foreground is the old Kent & Canterbury Hospital opened in 1793 and closed in 1937.*

This great abbey was founded by St. Augustine in AD597. Before the death of Becket and the building of his shrine, it rivalled the Cathedral in size and wealth. It was a place of pilgrimage with its religious relics and tombs of several early Christian saints. Archbishop Lanfranc started a major re-building and enlarging programme at the Abbey in 1070. In 1538 part of St. Augustine's was rebuilt by Henry VIII as a Royal palace. It became popular and in 1573 Elizabeth I had a lavish banquet here to celebrate her birthday. Later, Charles I and his bride Henrietta-Maria started their honeymoon here. The Abbey was then to go through a long period of decline and neglect and large portions of it were used as a quarry for new buildings elsewhere in the city. A brewery later used the buildings and the ground became a pleasure park which regularly held cock fights. In 1848, J. Beresford Hope, the MP for Maidstone, bought the abbey and rebuilt it as a missionary college. Today the abbey ruins are open to the public and the old college is part of the King's School.

BOTTOM LEFT: *The magnificent gateway to St. Augustine's Abbey shortly after the opening of the Missionary College in 1848.*

BOTTOM RIGHT: *A grand banquet was held in 1838 in the grounds to celebrate the anniversary of the Conservative Club.*

I n 1084 Archbishop Lanfranc founded the St. John's Hospital in Northgate, which with the St. Nicholas Hospital at nearby Harbledown shares the claim to being the oldest of their kind in the country. Just across the road from St. John's Lanfranc also founded St. Gregory's Priory which rivalled the Cathedral and St. Augustine's in size and importance. Northgate got its name from an ancient gateway which spanned the Reculver road near St. Mary's Church. The Mayor and Corporation would welcome Royalty here and present them with the keys to the city. Palace Street is named after the Archbishop's Palace built by Lanfranc. He demolished 27 houses to create this new street which still has the palace wall and gateway flanking one side. Palace Street contains many old timber-framed buildings, including Conquest House where the knights met the night before they murdered Archbishop Becket.

At the end of the 18th century three large barracks were built to the north of the area. The soldiers dramatically increased the population of Canterbury and they were to provide it with a great source of wealth. The city soon became the main military station for the Southern District of England and by 1815 more than 30,000 men were based here.

TOP: *This old house stands at 28 Palace St. In 1906 it was used as an antique shop; later it was to become the King's School shop. It has many fine carvings including a depiction of a Red Indian.*

BOTTOM: *In June 1910 Mr Henry Dawson flew his monoplane built of bamboo and steel from the old park, St. Martin's. Here he is shown proudly seated with onlookers prior to take-off.*

TOP: *This view of the Butter Market in 1904 shows some of the city's earliest automobiles by the Marlowe Memorial. In the background is the ruinous front of the Christchurch Gate. In 1935 it was restored and its turrets returned.*

OPPOSITE: *Mackenzie's view of the Butter Market in 1837 with part of the dome to the right of the picture.*
RIGHT: *Theobald & Studman's Model 'T' delivery van.*
BELOW: *This store stood opposite the gateway for many years.*

For much of the last century a large oval dome, supported on columns, covered part of this area and beneath it local farmers would bring their goods to sell. Then in 1888 the Butter Market was demolished and in its place the city erected a memorial to its best known literary son, Christopher Marlowe. The memorial, now in the Dane John Gardens, was unveiled by Henry Irving. Today, on the same spot, stands Canterbury's War Memorial, unveiled in 1921. The magnificent Christchurch Gateway, which leads to the cathedral precincts, was completed in 1517.

The Cathedral

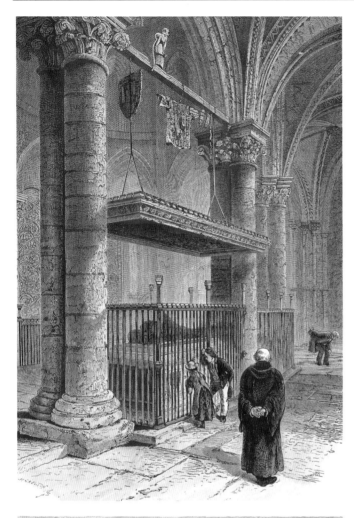

TOP: *Young Victorian children are seen here looking through the railings that surround the tomb of Edward, the Black Prince, on the south side of the Trinity Chapel. He was buried close to the shrine of St. Thomas Becket in 1376. Above his magnificent effigy hang his helmet, gauntlet and surcoat.*

BOTTOM: *On the 3 September 1872 a fire broke out on the roof of the cathedral's Trinity Chapel. This print shows members of the Canterbury Volunteer Fire Brigade dowsing the flames with their hoses.*

A ugustine founded a Cathedral here in 602, on what was probably an early Roman church. But his building was destroyed by fire shortly after the Norman Conquest, and between 1070 and 1077 Archbishop Lanfranc rebuilt it and the adjoining Monastery. The Cathedral's importance and Canterbury's fame grew dramatically after Thomas Becket's murder in 1170. His shrine was to become the most important outside the Holy Land. The pilgrims who came were from all walks of life and in special years they could number more than 100,000. In 1174 another fire destroyed part of the Cathedral and the great Norman architect, William of Sens, was to start the rebuilding. After a serious fall his place was taken by William the Englishman, who eventually finished the work. One of the country's great heroes, Edward the Black Prince – who at the age of 16 led the rout of the French at the Battle of Crécy – was buried on the south side of Becket's tomb in 1376. Henry IV and his Queen are also buried here. In 1538 Henry VIII declared Becket a traitor and rebel: his shrine was destroyed and its treasures plundered. Today, the Cathedral is again the focal point for millions of visitors from all over the world who come to admire both its beauty and history.

ABOVE: *One of the finest views of the cathedral was painted by the gifted King's School art teacher, Louis Raze, in 1846.*

WHEN THAT APRILLE WITH HIS SHOWERES SOOTE · THE DROUGHT OF MARCH HATH PIERCED TO THE ROOTE · THEN LONGEN FOLK

CANTERBU

PLACES of INTEREST

Roper Gateway .. 1.	⁓ The Precinct ⁓
House of Agnes ..2.	Christchurch Gate. 13.
S. Thomas Hospital. 3.	Archbishop's Palace.14.
Canterbury Weavers. 4.	The King's School. 15.
Blackfriars .... 5.	The Deanery .... 16.
S. John's Hospital ..6.	County War Memorial.17.
Grey Friars ..... 7.	⁓The City Gates⁓
Poor Priests Hosp ~. 8.	West Gate. . . . A
Queen Elizabeth's	North Gate. site .B
Guest Chamber~ 9.	Quenin Gate. " C
Chequers of the Hope.10.	Bur Gate. " D
Simon Langton Sch~	Newin Gate. " E
Austin Friars. site 11.	Riding Gate. " F
The Castle .....12.	Worth Gate. " G
The principal Hotels are named on the Map.	

THE BLACK PRINCE

A bird's eye view of Canterbury before the deva
of parts of the city in 1942

TO FERNE HALWES KNOWTHE IN SUNDRY LANDS · AND SPECIALLY · FROM · EVERY SHIRES END